Perf...
• Simp...

Fish

Deirdre McQuillan
ILLUSTRATED BY ALWYN GILLESPIE

Appletree Press

First published in 1992 by
The Appletree Press Ltd,
7 James Street South, Belfast BT2 8DL.
Copyright © 1992 The Appletree Press Ltd.
Printed in the E.C. All rights reserved.
No part of this publication may be reproduced or
transmitted in any form or by means, electronic or
mechanical, photocopying, recording or any
information and retrieval system, without
permission in writing from the publisher.

Perfectly Simple: Fish

A catalogue record for this book is available
from the British Library.

ISBN 0-86281-331-X

9 8 7 6 5 4 3 2 1

Acknowledgements

The author would like to thank Eamon Walsh and
Ross Lewis of The Old Dublin Restaurant for their
generosity and help, Anton Mosimann for permission
to reproduce his recipe for halibut; Mike Bunn,
Liz Ravaud, Hilary Brophy, Pat Scott and particularly
Paul Gillespie to whom this book is dedicated.

A note on measures

Imperial, metric and American measures have been
given for all recipes, which are for four people unless
otherwise stated.

Introduction

"God made food, the devil the cooks", wrote James Joyce in *Ulysses*. Many people are put off cooking fish by penitential memories of boiled haddock or fried whiting. Yet the pleasures of eating a freshly caught wild salmon, the briny taste of an oyster, the aroma of a trout grilling over an open fire are the stuff of music, poetry and song. Fish, rich in vitamins, minerals and protein, is the least spoiled of all our foods, yet it is the one that spoils the fastest. The secret of culinary success is always to insist on the freshest fish in season. And never overcook it. Then there are all the varieties – and it's worth going to a fish market just to see them – many of which never reach the shops.

Alan Davidson's magisterial *North Atlantic Seafood* lists nearly 200 species of edible fish in the vast realms of that ocean. These days luxury fish are globetrotters that travel first class to satisfy the gourmet palate. I've seen farmed sea bass from America on sale in Dublin: fish farming is only in its infancy.

The recipes in this book are mostly simple and elementary, but their techniques can be applied to many other types of fish and may inspire an enthusiast to trawl further afield. In the meantime, get hooked on a good fishmonger, learn how to look a fresh fish straight in the eye and get off to a frying start!

Basic Fish Stock

This is simple to make and can be frozen (like ice cubes and then bagged) for use when needed. It is the basis for many soups, pies and sauces. Some experts say that sole and flounder make the best stock, but ask your fishmonger for a selection of fish.

2–3 lbs/900g – 1 1/2 kg of fish bones
trimmings, heads and skin
1 whole onion, sliced
1 carrot, chopped
1 stick of celery, chopped including base
1 tbsp wine vinegar
1 glass of white wine
2 1/2 – 3 pts/500–600 fl oz/5–6 cups cold water
10 whole peppercorns
bouquet garni

Wash off any remaining blood from the fish under a tap. In a large pot, put in the cold water and the fish pieces, bring to the boil, skimming occasionally. Now add the rest of the ingredients, cover and allow to simmer for 30 minutes. Strain, return strained liquid to the pot and boil hard for about 15 minutes to reduce stock by about 1/3. Do not add salt. When cool, it can be frozen and kept until needed.

Fish Soup

A rich, colourful and nutritious soup that is a meal in itself.
It can be frozen successfully too, and if desired you can
leave out the mussels.

2 tbsp butter
3 carrots, sliced
2 sticks celery, chopped
1 leek, cleaned and chopped
5 mangetout, chopped
1 lb/450g potatoes chopped in ¹/₂ in/1 cm cubes
10 fl oz/300ml fish stock
1 glass of white wine
3 fl oz/80ml cream
1 lb/450g cod fillets, cut into chunks
12 scrubbed and bearded mussels
salt and pepper
chopped parsley

Melt butter in a pot and soften the vegetables (not the
potatoes) for about 5 minutes. Add potatoes and soften
in the butter for about 3 minutes. Add fish stock, white
wine and cream, bring to the boil and simmer until
potatoes are cooked, about 15–20 minutes. Now add the
cod and simmer about 3 minutes, then add mussels, cover
and simmer for another 2–3 minutes. Season with salt
and pepper, stir in chopped parsley and serve (in a
warmed tureen) with chunks of fresh white bread.

Smokies

A perfect start to a dinner party for 6, tangy and appetising and a breeze to make.

1 medium onion, chopped
2 oz/50g/¹/₂ stick butter
10oz/275g smoked trout fillets
4 large tomatoes
8oz/225g grated cheese
(hard and herby, such as Cotswold)
juice of 1 lemon
¹/₂ tsp sugar
salt and pepper

Pre-heat oven to gas mark 6, 400°F, 200°C. Peel and chop onions and sweat them in butter until soft and golden. Break up trout into big bite-size pieces. Core the tomatoes and plunge into boiling water for a few minutes, then into cold water and peel off skin, de-seed and chop. Grate about 6oz/175g of the cheese, retain the rest for sprinkling on top. Mix all the ingredients together in a bowl, add lemon juice, sugar and season to taste. Divide this mixture into 6 ramekin dishes, sprinkle with the remaining cheese and bake until brown and bubbling, about 15–20 minutes.

Mussel and Potato Salad

A detailed recipe for this dish was once given in a play by Alexander Dumas, calling for a glass of Château d'Yquem with instructions for surrounding the dish with truffles cooked in champagne! For some reason it has often been known as a Japanese salad; either way it is the most delicious cold (or warm) salad whose success lies in the way in which the warm potatoes absorb the flavours of the wine, the herbs and the vinaigrette.

2 ¼ lb/1 kg mussels
4 sprigs parsley
4 fl oz/110 ml white wine
1 stick of celery, chopped
6 peppercorns, crushed
1½ lb/750g potatoes
1 tbsp thyme, chopped
2 shallots, chopped
1 tbsp parsley, chopped
3 tbsp white wine vinegar (Orleans or tarragon)
6 tbsp olive oil
3 tsp Dijon mustard
1 glass Noilly Prat or White Martini (dry vermouth)

Put the clean, scrubbed and bearded mussels in a deep pot with white wine, parsley sprigs, celery and peppercorns. Cover and bring to the boil for a couple of minutes until the mussels open. Remove mussels from their shells and set them aside to cool. Whizz the olive oil, wine vinegar

and the mustard in a blender and set aside. Boil the
potatoes in the mussel juices and water and when they are
cooked, peel quickly while still hot and slice thickly into
a large bowl. At the same time, mix in the vermouth and
then the chopped fresh herbs and finally toss in the
vinaigrette and the mussels. Serve immediately sprinkled
with chopped parsley or leave to chill, covered, in a
refrigerator.

Angels on Horseback

Being Irish, I think the best way to eat a host of Galway
oysters is *au naturel* with a dash of lemon juice, plenty of
buttered brown bread and Guinness. These old favourites,
however, make a party snack or appetiser and are a good
introduction to cooked oysters for those who have never
tasted them before.

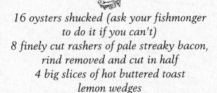

*16 oysters shucked (ask your fishmonger
to do it if you can't)
8 finely cut rashers of pale streaky bacon,
rind removed and cut in half
4 big slices of hot buttered toast
lemon wedges*

Pre-heat grill. Drain oysters and pat dry. Wind a piece of
streaky bacon around each oyster and skewer with a
wooden toothpick or cocktail stick. Grill on both sides
until the bacon is brown and crispy and serve with the hot
buttered toast and lemon wedges.

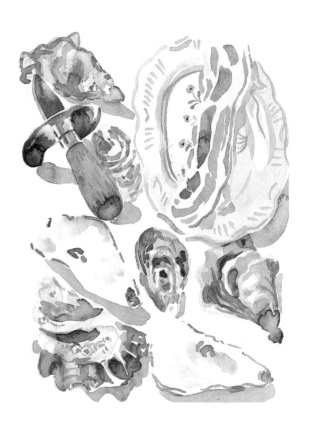

Crab Pâté

8oz/225g fresh crabmeat
4oz/110g/1 stick butter, softened
1 shallot, finely chopped
1 tbsp parsley, chopped
1 clove of garlic, crushed
ground pepper
pinch cayenne pepper
lemon juice to taste
2 fl oz/50ml fish stock
1 tbsp tomato and courgette chutney (Sharwoods)
chopped fresh herbs for garnish such as
chives, parsley, chervil

Blend crabmeat with the butter, shallot, parsley, garlic, cayenne, pepper, lemon juice, fish stock and chutney in a blender or food processor. Check seasoning to taste. Press the mixture into a bowl, cover and chill. Alternatively, roll it like a sausage in greaseproof paper, twisting the ends and chill. Before serving, roll it over a bed of chopped fresh herbs such as chives, parsley, or chervil to cover. Good with thin slices of hot buttered toast or brown bread and lemon wedges.

Smoked Haddock Mousse

The best smoked haddock is said to come from Scotland where specialty methods of curing the haddock developed. Now they are widespread. This makes a good light supper dish or the starter to a meal.

1 lb/500g smoked haddock fillets
5 fl oz/150ml milk
1 carrot, sliced
1 onion, sliced
few parsley stalks, bay leaf, sprig of thyme
2 cloves of garlic, crushed
1 fl oz/30ml cream
2 egg yolks
3 fl oz/90ml olive oil
juice of 1/2 lemon
salt and pepper

Put the haddock, milk, carrot, onion, garlic, bay leaf, parsley and thyme in a pot, heat and poach for 10 minutes. Cool and flake the fish, removing any skin and bones. Chop up the fish, add the cream and egg yolks, mix well. Dribble in the oil in a thin stream until the mixture looks like mashed potato. Season to taste. Add lemon juice and serve hot or cold with buttered toast.

Moules Marinière

This is one of the great dishes from the Atlantic coast of France where it appears on nearly every restaurant menu. On the west coast of Ireland, it is a regular "free" meal when we go to the rocks at low tide to collect the mussels hidden under curtains of slippery seaweed. It can make a light starter course or a main meal.

4 lbs/1 1/2 kg mussels, cleaned, scrubbed and bearded
2oz/50g/1/2 stick butter
2 shallots, finely chopped
1 stick of celery, chopped
1 tsp thyme, chopped
1 bay leaf
a few twists of ground pepper
1 glass of white wine

Clean and beard the mussels under running water discarding any that are open or seem unduly heavy. In a deep pot, heat the butter and sweat the shallots, celery, thyme, bay leaf and pepper for about 2–3 minutes on a low heat. Turn up heat, add a generous glass of wine and boil a minute or two, then add the mussels, cover tightly and boil quickly on a high heat for about 2 minutes until the mussels open, shaking the pot a couple of times lightly. Garnish with parsley. Eat with your fingers, using an empty shell to pinch out the mussels, and provide finger bowls. Mop up the juice with lots of crusty bread or provide soup spoons.

Soused Herrings

Maybe it's the line of a song, but it always comes into my head when the subject of herrings comes up. "God bless us and save us," said old Mrs Davis, "I never knew herrings was fish." A lovely, delicate soused herring is a great way to start the day.

4 fresh herrings, filleted
1 medium onion, sliced
2 bay leaves
2 tsp pickling spice
equal parts white malt vinegar and water
salt and pepper

Pre-heat oven to gas mark 2, 300°F, 150°C. Rub the herring fillets with salt all over. Put them in an ovenproof dish and add the sliced onion, pickling spice and bay leaves and cover with the malt vinegar and water. Cover with tin foil and bake for approximately 40 minutes. Allow to cool. Serve with brown bread and butter.

Gravlax

One of the great delicacies of Norway, gravlax (literally "grave" salmon) is an ancient method of curing salmon in pre-refrigeration days. Some cooks suggest that it is better to deep freeze the salmon for a day before preparation to kill any bacteria.

1 lb/500g tail-end fillet of wild salmon, freed from
bones but with skin intact
1 tbsp sugar
1 tbsp white pepper, roughly ground
1 tbsp coarse sea salt
3 tbsp fresh dill, chopped

Place fillet on a piece of foil, skin side down. Sprinkle with sugar, then layer with crushed white peppercorns, sea salt and finally the chopped dill. Fold the foil like an envelope and leave it in a fridge for 48 hours with a weight on top. To serve, scrape off the marinade with a knife and slice thinly, as for smoked salmon, using a straight-edged carving knife, working diagonally with the grain towards the tail. Cubed potatoes, lightly cooked in cream, with the addition of some fresh dill and a dash of lemon juice, make a good accompaniment, or serve as for smoked salmon, with brown bread and lemon wedges.

Ceviche

A method of "cold cooking" raw fish in lime or lemon juice, *ceviche* is said to be of Polynesian origin for which the recipe was first written down in the 1930s. It is one that has been adopted enthusiastically in Mexican cuisine with added ingredients like hot chillies and peppers to spice it up. It can be made with other fish such as sole or mackerel though "cooking" times are variable. It is best with scallops as it preserves the incomparable delicate taste of the shellfish.

*8 king scallops removed from their shells and cleaned
(your fishmonger can do this for you)
lime or lemon juice to cover
3 tbsp olive oil
salt and pepper
salad greens such as lettuce, oak leaf, lamb's lettuce
chopped herbs such as chives and parsley, or fresh
coriander on its own
a few drops of Tabasco (optional)*

Slice the scallops into coins and place them in a glass or ceramic bowl in a bath of lime or lemon juice to cover completely. Marinate for 2 hours turning occasionally. Drain. Mix 1½–2 tbsp of this juice with the olive oil, season to taste and add chopped fresh coriander or parsley and chives. Toss the scallops in this mixture and place on a bed of mixed salad greens.

Ray in Black Butter

Black butter sauce actually dates back to the sixteenth century and this dish is one of the classics of French cuisine. This recipe has a major difference in that the ray is simmered in the white wine vinegar, without the usual addition of water, which concentrates the taste. You can substitute skate for ray.

2 large ray wings
2 fl oz/50ml white wine vinegar
1 clove of garlic , crushed
1 onion, finely chopped
2oz/50g/^{1}/$_2$ stick butter
capers and chopped parsley to garnish
(serves 2)

You need a large and a small frying pan for this dish. First wash the fish and pat dry. In a wide frying pan heat the vinegar, garlic and onion and add the fish. Cook for 10 minutes on a low heat turning several times. Remove the fish from the pan, leaving the juices behind. Scrape off the thin covering membrane with a knife and then remove the flesh from each side of the wings and place in a warm dish. In a smaller frying pan heat the butter until it is brown (watch very carefully that it doesn't go black) and quickly pour over the fish. Now transfer the juices from the first pan to the second, boil fiercely for a few seconds and pour over the fish. Decorate with parsley and capers and serve with fried courgettes or stir-fried broccoli.

Cod Stuffed with Spinach

A hearty, inexpensive family dish that can be prepared quickly. Fresh spinach can be used instead of frozen, but it takes a little longer. Blanch 1 lb/500g fresh, cleaned spinach in boiling water for 3 minutes, drain completely and chop.

1 medium onion
2 sticks of celery
2oz/50g/¹/₂ stick butter
2 x 11oz/300g packages of frozen spinach, defrosted
4 cod fillets
1 fishstock cube (or 10 fl oz fish stock)
10 fl oz/275ml cream
2–3oz/50–75g grated Emmenthal cheese

Pre-heat oven to gas mark 4, 350°F, 180°C. Chop onion and celery finely and fry in butter until onion is transparent. Add spinach, blend with onion and celery and cook for 2 minutes. Place spinach, onion and celery on the base of a wide baking dish with the cod fillets on top. Blend stock cube with 3 tbsp boiling water until fully dissolved, then add cream. Pour over dish, season to taste with salt and pepper and sprinkle grated cheese on top. Bake for 25 minutes.

Seafood Pasta

Seafood goes well with pasta and this dish is a complete meal in itself. Try to time the cooking so that the pasta is ready just before the sauce.

8oz/250g prawns
or shrimps
3 tbsp olive oil
1oz/25g/$\frac{1}{4}$ stick butter
1 shallot, finely chopped
2 cloves of garlic, peeled
and finely chopped
2 tbsp parsley, chopped
2 tbsp thyme, chopped
1 tsp salt

10 fl oz/275ml cream
4 fl oz/125ml white wine
1 lb/500g clean, scrubbed
and bearded mussels
8oz/250g scallops,
shucked and sliced
into coins
1 lb/500g tagliatelle
(fresh if possible)

Plunge the prawns or shrimps into boiling salted water for several minutes until cooked. Put them in iced water to cool, then peel and set aside. Prepare boiling salted water (with a little drop of oil) for the pasta, and cook *al dente* while the sauce is in preparation. Heat the butter and olive oil in a large frying pan and sauté the shallots and garlic until soft on a low heat. Add the wine, cream, thyme, parsley and salt. Boil for 8–10 minutes until it has a thick consistency, then add the sliced scallops and cook for 1 minute. Add the mussels. Cover and cook for 2–3 minutes until they open. Finally, stir in the prawns to warm them through. At this stage your pasta should be ready; put it in a large serving dish and pour the whole mixture over it. Serve immediately.

Grey Mullet with Bacon and Sage

This is a recipe from Jane Grigson's *Fish Cookery* which we have made many times. A silvery-scaled fish that somewhat resembles the sea bass, the mullet is an inshore feeder which gets its sustenance from herbs rather than other small fish. The little thumbnail-like scales get all over the place when you remove them, so try to do it over a large piece of newspaper.

3 x 1 lb grey mullet	3oz/75g/³/₄ stick butter
6 rashers of smoked back bacon	4–5 fl oz/150ml dry vermouth
12 sage leaves	salt and pepper
2oz/50g breadcrumbs	4 fl oz/120ml cream

Pre-heat oven to gas mark 6, 400°F, 200°C. Scale and clean the mullet and slash in 4 or 5 places on each side. Chop the bacon and sage leaves finely together. Fill the slashes with a little of this paste. Mix the rest with the breadcrumbs, season well and stuff into the cavities of the fish. Butter a baking dish lavishly and arrange the mullet side by side. Bake in a fairly hot oven for 15 minutes. Pour over the vermouth and return to the oven for another 10–15 minutes until done. Pour over the cream and leave for another 2 minutes in the oven. Serve immediately.

Lobster

For two people, this is the ultimate luxurious, but simple treat that needs no introduction. Rich and rare.

1 x ³/₄–1 lb/300g lobster
butter
lemon juice
black pepper, ground
(serves 2)

Plunge the lobster into boiling salted water for 15 minutes. Allow to cool. Remove the claws and flippers. Crack the large claws with a nutcracker to extract the flesh. Using a heavy knife with a sharp point, cut through the entire length of the lobster body and tail. Spread open and remove the meat. The green part is tomalley, or liver, which is edible as is the red part – the coral – or roe. Discard other parts. Clean two sections of the body shell and reserve. Now put the lobster meat back into the shells and paint with melted butter and lemon juice and sprinkle with black pepper. Serve with fresh asparagus.

Dublin Lawyer An often-quoted recipe for lobster from the late Theodora Fitzgibbon, the distinguished Irish food writer.

Remove all meat from the cooked lobster. Cut the meat into chunks, heat some butter until foaming and gently heat the lobster meat in it. Warm 4 tablespoons whiskey slightly, then pour into the pan and set it alight (stand back!). Remove lobster to a warm serving dish and keep warm. Add 5 fl oz/150ml of cream to the pan, mix with the pan juices and season. Boil hard for a couple of minutes to reduce the sauce by half, stir in the lobster and serve at once in the shells.

Grilled Mackerel with Gooseberry Sauce

4 fresh mackerel fillets
1 lb/250g gooseberries, washed, topped and tailed
Parsley butter:
4oz/100g/1 stick softened butter
handful of finely chopped parsley
seasonings
1 tsp lemon juice

Pre-heat grill. Line a grill rack with tin foil (as the mackerel is inclined to stick) or butter the grill pan. Slash the fillets twice across and lay the skin skinside down. Mix the ingredients for the parsley butter and paint this onto the fish. Grill for about 1–2 minutes, then reduce heat. Baste again with the butter and continue until fish is cooked. Make the sauce by stewing the gooseberries with a little water until they burst. Add a little bit of sugar to taste and push through a sieve, adding, if liked, a few drops of ginger squeezed through a garlic press.

Fish Cakes

A good way of using leftovers and one that is popular with children. You could substitute cod or hake for the salmon.

¹/₂ lb/225g cooked salmon, free of bones and flaked
¹/₂ lb/225g potatoes, boiled and sieved
1 tbsp chives, chopped
1 tbsp parsley, chopped
2 beaten eggs
seasoned flour
2oz/50g breadcrumbs
1oz/30g/¹/₄ stick butter
salt and freshly ground pepper

Mix the salmon, potatoes, chives, parsley and seasonings and add one beaten egg to bind. Form into cakes or patties about 1 in / 30mm thick, roll in flour, dip in beaten egg, shaking off surplus, then coat in breadcrumbs. Heat butter in the pan and fry on both sides until golden.

Gambas a la Plancha

This is the quickest and most delicious way to eat Dublin Bay prawns, or large shrimps, cooked the way they do it in Cadiz in southern Spain in a heavy flat-bottomed skillet or griddle.

Salt prawns, leaving them whole. Heat the griddle or skillet until so hot that a drop of water will sizzle instantly. Then film it with olive oil and quickly fry the prawns for

2 minutes on each side. Serve immediately with lemon wedges, finger bowls, and plenty of chunky fresh white bread. Messy, but worth it.

Oyster Loaf (*La Médiatrice*)

An eighteenth-century English dish, the oyster loaf became popular in New Orleans at the end of the nineteenth century and it is said to be what unfaithful Creole husbands gave their wives when they wanted to say "sorry". It is also known in Louisiana as an Oyster "Po' Boy".

1 stick of French bread, or baguette, cut in half
2oz/50g/¼ stick butter
24 small oysters, shucked
cornflour
2 tbsp olive oil
shredded lettuce
mayonnaise, preferably homemade

Pre-heat oven to gas mark 7, 425°F, 220°C. Scoop out the bread from the bottom part of the loaf, brush both halves with melted butter and bake for about 15–20 minutes until brown. (Alternatively you could put them under a hot grill.) Dip the drained oysters in cornflour and fry in hot olive oil for about 2½ minutes. Drain on kitchen paper. Fill the hollowed-out shell with the oysters, top with some shredded lettuce and mayonnaise, then close

with the other half. Serve in hot slices with guacamole sauce and cold beer.

Pan-Fried Tuna with Fresh Herbs

To anyone who has only ever experienced tinned tuna, the taste of the fresh fish, which is more like a meat both in colour and texture, comes as an agreeable surprise. This is a fast dish, full of flavour. The herbs which add fragrance to the oil can be varied according to season.

1½ lbs/675g tuna fillets (preferably bonito)
1oz/30g/¼ stick butter
4 tbsp olive oil
2 cloves of garlic, crushed
3 tbsp fresh chopped herbs, such as winte
savoury, rosemary, thyme
parsley and/or lemon balm to garnish

Slice the fillets very thinly (to ⅛ in or 3 mm approx). In a bowl add 2 tbsp of olive oil to the garlic and coat the fillets in it. Heat the remaining olive oil and the butter in a large frying pan and toss in the chopped herbs, sautéing lightly for 1 minute. Turn up heat, add fillets and fry for approximately 3 minutes, turning them gently from time to time. Serve with pan juices and sprinkle with chopped fresh herbs such as lemon balm or parsley. Pan-fried potatoes and courgettes accompany this dish well.

Plaice à la Meunière

This was a regular Friday dish when I was growing up and the fish was sold fresh from a delivery van that toured the neighbourhood in the mornings. It is quick, though tricky, and it is imperative that the fish be absolutely fresh. Because the average frying pan can only hold about 3 medium-size fillets, this recipe is for 2.

3 plaice fillets
seasoned flour
1oz/25g/2 tbsp clarified butter for frying
1oz/25g/¼ stick butter
lemon juice
chopped parsley
(serves 2)

Dust the plaice fillets in seasoned flour. Heat the clarified butter in a frying pan, then quickly fry the fish on each side until it is nicely browned. Transfer fish to warmed plates. Pour off excess butter from pan, give it a quick wipe with kitchen paper, then add the fresh (unclarified) butter and heat until brown but not black. You must watch carefully at this point. Quickly add lemon juice and pour over the plaice. Garnish with chopped fresh parsley. Serve with mashed potatoes and spinach.

Clarified Butter Heat 8oz/225g of butter and simmer gently until all the moisture has evaporated; this can take up to half an hour. When the foam has become brown and crusty, poke aside with a spoon and strain butter through

muslin or a metal coffee filter into a wide-brimmed container (not plastic). Refrigerated and covered it will keep for weeks. Makes approx. 6 fl oz/150ml.

Salmon en Papillote

A perfect dinner-party dish that can be made with either steaks or fillets of salmon. Its success lies in the succulence of the fish derived from the conserving juices and the array of colours from the surrounding vegetables.

olive oil
1 leek, thinly sliced
(the white part)
4 salmon steaks or fillets
1oz/25g/¼ stick butter
12 cherry tomatoes
cut in half

sliced julienne strips of
green, red and
yellow peppers
juice of 1 lemon
1 glass of Noilly Prat/
dry white vermouth
salt and pepper
parsley

Pre-heat oven to gas mark 6–8, 400–450°F, 200–230°C. Cut heavy foil into four 12 in x 12 in / 300 mm x 300 mm pieces. Brush each with a tablespoon of olive oil and layer with a bed of leeks. Lay the salmon on the leeks and put a knob of butter on top. Arrange the tomatoes and strips of peppers around the salmon and add lemon juice, vermouth and season with salt and pepper. Scatter with parsley. Fold up the foil tightly at the edges leaving plenty of space and bake on a baking tray for 15 minutes. Serve with wild rice or new potatoes and mangetout.

Monkfish with Curry, Lemon and Ginger Sauce

The sweet, succulent, dense flesh of the monkfish has often been called the poor man's lobster. Like its majestic crustacean colleague, it feeds on shellfish. Its terrifyingly grotesque head belies a sublime-tasting flesh. It has to be carefully cooked as it toughens if overcooked. It also makes an ideal fish for kebabs.

2 lbs/1 kg monkfish fillets, thinly sliced	1 tsp curry paste (Sharwoods)
olive oil	2 bay leaves
1 clove of garlic, crushed	pinch turmeric
sliced peeled ginger	10 fl oz/300ml cream
10 fl oz/300ml fish stock	ground white pepper
1 glass of dry vermouth	salt
lemon juice	

Cut fillets into pieces and leave to marinate in a mixture of 2 tablespoons olive oil, garlic, and a few slices of fresh ginger. Heat a thin film of olive oil in a frying pan and add the monkfish, frying lightly for about 20 seconds to seal. Drain off excess oil, add fish stock, vermouth, lemon juice (to taste), curry paste, bay leaves and turmeric and poach for 2–3 minutes. Remove the monkfish with a slotted spoon, place on a warm dish. Boil sauce rapidly for 3–4 minutes until it is of coating consistency. Season to taste. Serve with mashed potatoes studded with chopped fresh chives.

Prawns in Garlic Butter

One of the best seafood restaurants in Ireland, Ahern's of
Youghal in Co. Cork has featured this dish on its menu for
over 20 years, and it never loses its popularity. It can be
served either as a first course with 6 prawns per person or
12 for a main course. Cholesterol watchers, beware, this
is a sinful pleasure.

24 large raw Dublin Bay prawn tails
salt
fresh breadcrumbs
1 lb/400g/4 sticks butter (you may have some left over)
2 small garlic bulbs, the cloves peeled and crushed
5 fl oz/150ml red wine
2 tbsp mixed fresh herbs, chopped
freshly ground pepper
1 onion, finely diced

Pre-heat oven to gas mark 6, 400°F, 200°C. Place the
prawns in a large saucepan of boiling salted water. When
they float to the top in a couple of minutes, remove and
place in iced water. Shell when cool. Whizz the softened
butter, garlic, red wine, chopped herbs, pepper and onion
in a blender. Place a little of this mixture in each hole of
an escargot or small ovenproof dish and put a prawn on
top. Cover the prawn with more butter and sprinkle
breadcrumbs on top. Place the escargot dishes in the oven
for approximately 10–15 minutes. Serve hot with garlic
bread.

Fish Pie with Parsley and Potatoes

An inexpensive, nutritious family dish that needs no accompaniment, this fish pie can be prepared in advance.

15 fl oz/425ml milk
4 cod or haddock cutlets or fillets (about 1¹/₂ lb/675g)
1¹/₂ oz/40g/¹/₂ stick butter
1¹/₂ oz/40g flour
1 shallot, chopped
salt and pepper
juice of 1 lemon
good fistful of chopped fresh parsley
8 medium-size potatoes

Pre-heat oven to gas mark 6, 400°F, 200°C. Heat the milk gently in a saucepan and season. Add the fish and poach gently for about 5 minutes until the flesh comes off the bone easily. Strain and reserve liquid. To make the roux: heat the butter in a saucepan and then add chopped shallot and fry lightly. Add the flour and the strained milk slowly and stir until it thickens in about 5 minutes. Then throw in the parsley, cook gently for a further 2 minutes, adding the fish, salt and pepper to taste and finally the juice of a lemon. Put the mixture in a dish and top with cooked, mashed potatoes to which a little milk and butter have been added. Dot top with a little butter and bake for about 20 minutes in a hot oven.

Goujons of Halibut with Turnip, Orange and Basil

An elegant, colourful dish that is light and fat free, created by Anton Mosimann. In the eighteenth century, oranges were used to flavour fish as lemons are used today.

1¹/₂ lb/600g halibut fillets, skinned, boned and cut into
goujons (or fingers) of about ¹/₂ oz/15g each
salt and freshly ground pepper
¹/₂ tsp/2.5ml orange peel, finely chopped and blanched
5 fl oz/150ml fish stock
³/₄ oz/20g shallot, finely chopped
3 ¹/₂ oz/90g peeled turnips, cut into strips and blanched
8 basil leaves, torn into strips
12 orange segments

Season the fillets of halibut with salt, pepper and orange peel. Put the fish stock and shallots into a casserole, add the halibut, cover and poach gently on top of the stove for about 2 minutes. Remove the fish with a slotted spoon and keep warm. Boil the stock and reduce by ¹/₃. Add the turnips and basil and season to taste. Simmer for about 30 seconds; the turnips should be crunchy. Take a little stock out of the pan and place in a small separate pan. Warm the peeled orange segments in this. To serve, place the *goujons* in a suitable serving dish with the turnips and basil and cover with the well-seasoned stock.

Fish and Chip Salad

This original recipe is the brainchild of a Michelin star chef, Paul Rankin of Northern Ireland, who trained in London with the Roux brothers, then ran an hotel in the Nappa Valley in California, and now has his own restaurant "Roscoff" back in Belfast. For this starting course he combines an old favourite, fish and chips, with salad leaves and a tangy dressing.

1 lb/450g fresh snapper fillets (or haddock)
mixed salad leaves such as oak leaf,
lollo rosso or iceberg
2 large baking potatoes 12–14oz/350–400g
4 fl oz/100ml light olive oil
3 fl oz/70ml lemon juice or wine vinegar
1 tbsp Dijon mustard
1 tsp crushed garlic
vegetable oil for deep frying
olive oil for frying fish

Peel potatoes and cut into $1/4$ in / 25mm thick chips. Heat the vegetable oil in a deep saucepan until hot, but not boiling, and blanch the chips for 3–4 minutes. Drain the chips and reserve. Whizz the light olive oil, lemon juice, mustard and garlic in a blender. Heat the vegetable oil again until boiling and deep fry the chips until golden (this happens very quickly). Drain. Heat a large, heavy frying pan with a little olive oil until hot and smoking. Add the fillets carefully and sear them for approx. $1^1/2$ minutes on each side until they have a good colour. Remove from heat. Arrange the salad leaves and chips on a warm plate, add the

fillets. Pour the sauce from the blender into the hot pan, shake once and toss over the fish. Serve immediately.

How to Grill or Barbecue a Whole Fish

Clean and gut fish, but leave on the head. Leave on the scales if you want to eat the fish off the skin, remove scales (with the blunt edge of a knife by pushing backwards against them) if you want to eat the skin. Fish should be at room temperature before cooking starts. A charcoal fire should be grey and very hot. For medium to large fish (2–3 lbs / 900g – 1.5 kg) make a few diagonal slashes on each side for faster cooking. Mix in a cup of marinade of 2 tablespoons olive oil and 1 tablespoon lemon juice, salt and pepper with chopped fresh herbs such as thyme, dill or fennel. Paint this on the fish inside and out and place some extra herbs in the cavity. Use an oiled double-hinged wire rack for large and small fish to enable you to turn the fish.

The oilier the fish, the longer it takes to cook, but in general, with fish 6"–8" / 15–20 cm from the fire, small fish take 6–7 minutes, medium fish 8–12 minutes, but add 2–3 minutes if it's an oily fish. Large fish can take up to 30–45 minutes depending on oiliness. Keep basting throughout (if you put a spray of thyme in the marinade, it can be used like a brush) and sprinkle salt and pepper on each side of the fish when it is done. For fish kebabs, marinate the fish pieces for about 2 hours before cooking. Allow about 8–10 minutes for cooking. For steaks, such as swordfish, marinate for 2 hours, and add aromatic herbs to the fire; grill, basting, for 20 minutes.

Index